SAM LOVETT

American Squirrel

SAM LOVETT was a student at the Boston University School of Theology in 2016 when this collection was written during trips to Washington, DC, to visit Grace Palmer, the author's wife. This poetry was edited for publication by the author in 2025. Sam and Grace now live in Concord, NH, at St. Paul's School where Sam teaches humanities and works as a chaplain.

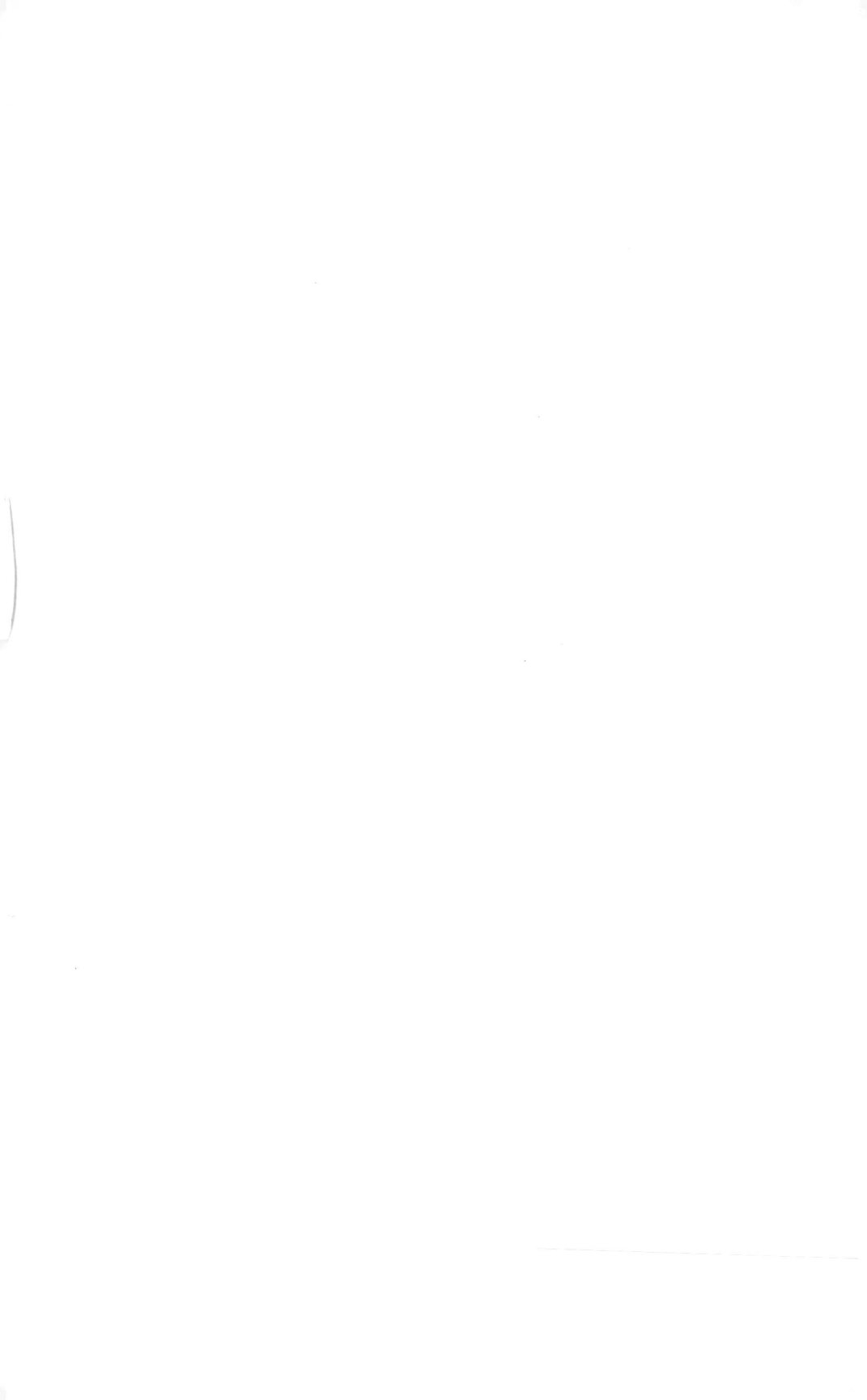

American Squirrel

Also by Sam Lovett

Petrus

Olim Quarters

American Squirrel

Sam Lovett

BELL PULL PRESS
Providence · 2025

Copyright © 2025 by Sam Lovett

All rights reserved. Published in the United States by Bell Pull Press. Except for brief quotations in critical articles or reviews, no part of this book may be reproduced in any manner without prior written permission from the publisher.

bellpullpress.com

Published in January 2025 by Bell Pull Press.
Printed in the United States of America.

Lovett, Sam
    American squirrel / Sam Lovett.
    ISBN: 979-8-9922773-2-6 (paperback)
    ISBN: 979-8-9922773-3-3 (hardcover)
    LCCN: 2025900200

The text of this book is set in Jensen Pro.

Epigraph on page 31 from "Remembering the Great Squirrel Purge of Lafayette Square," by John Kelly was first printed in *The Washington Post* on April 10, 2016. Reprinted with permission.

Epigraph on page 34 from "Squirrels, Friends Go Nuts in Their 'Digs' At Lafayette Square," by George Clifford was first printed in *The Washington Post* on June 20, 1984. Reprinted with permission.

10 9 8 7 6 5 4

Published by Bell Pull Press
Providence, RI

For Grace

*Permit me to once more trouble you about
my little friends the squirrels . . .*

*We have become great friends, and I feel
a great deal of interest in their welfare,
as they are nice little fellows.*

—George A. Gustin,
Treasury Department,
Washington, DC
(1903)

Contents

Preface xi
American Squirrel 1

I.
The Interrogation of Charlie Ferguson 5
Squirrels of Washington I 7
Henrie Introduced 8
The Park for Little Wanderers 9
The Curators 10
A Fashion of Birth 12
In the Public Garden 13
Interregnum 14
Walking Home from the Library of Congress 15
Recovery Day 16
Henrie at Trashcan 17
Vertiginous 18

II.
Watermill 23
I Worked at Lady's on Wednesday 24
House Money 26
Untitled 27
The Loop 28
H Street 30
Squirrels of Washington II 31
Lafayette Park 34
Space High 35
Aerial Artist 36
Henrie's Favorite 37
Sometimes I Make Lists Because I Don't Want
    to Forget Anything 38

Emelia   40
Hymns For Rachel   41

III.
Plumbago   47
The Squirrel is Legion   48
Animal Desire   49
My First Summer in the Silicon   50
Cubs Win World Series, Four Games to Three   51
Coffee   52
Christopher Wren Dances in Anacostia   53
Metrophysics   54
Squirrels of Washington III   55
Greater Than Me   56
Capitol Hill Classic   57
Offshoots   58
Radio Waves   59
Hypotheosis   60
(Jo-Lonn) Dunbar Theater   61
I'll Be Seeing You (Henrie's Song)   62
Election   63
Compilation   64
Mrs. Frisby and the Rats   65
Traceur   66
The Machine   67
Imperfect Mirror   68
In A Different Key, Gatsby   69
My Dear Sir   70
America's Front Yard: An Echo   72

Notes   74
Indices   79

Preface

In Washington, DC, influence is a matter of altitude (p. 34). In 1910, Congress capped the height of DC buildings by passing the "Height of Buildings Act." Today only five buildings in the city exceed two-hundred feet: two churches, an office building, a hotel, and the United States Capitol. Among the animals in the city, squirrels live at the top, limited only by how high the canopy will take them.

Why this interest in squirrels? Squirrels seem to be a throughline connecting many topics I think are important: good government, a healthy environment, American history and humanities ... perhaps you will agree—or not—after reading *American Squirrel*. In my life I've lived in several places where squirrels are widespread; they make their presence known. One of my earliest poems was about a squirrel (or raccoon?) who was stuck in the attic of my apartment in 2010. Their daring feats amaze me (p. 28). I respect their audacity.

I wrote most of these poems in 2016 during a precipitous hinge year in American civic life. I was fortunate to spend so much time that year working at the Library of Congress and visiting the Smithsonian museums and archives, thinking about what actions I would take in my own life to be a force for the common good (p. 14). Several years later, January 2025 feels like an appropriate moment to be editing and publishing these poems as the same precarious hinge is groaning—screeching madly, pinching dangerously.

From a different perspective, these were good years for the squirrels. The years 2016 and 2025 abutted *mast years* on the East Coast, meaning the trees in the region shifted their energy to overproduce an abundance of flowers and seeds. As a result, good acorns have been sown; the squirrels are fed; future trees are on the way to raise us to a higher plane—if we can stabilize, if we can cultivate, if we can find a way to live in the park, together (p. 9). I hope you enjoy these poems.

S. L.

New Hampshire
January 2025

Figure 1. Watercolor on graphite of squirrel and eagle, by Giacinto Capelli, c. 1939. National Gallery of Art.

American Squirrel

> *The urbanization of the gray squirrel in the United States between the mid-nineteenth century and the early twentieth century was an ecological and cultural process that changed the squirrels' ways of life.*
> —Etienne Benson

The bald eagle is an imperfect American
symbol. We are not eagles—rare, regal birds.
We are squirrels—prolific mammals,
urban daredevils. The squirrel is a thief and hoarder.

The squirrel is a survivor. It regenerates its
environment. It is ever-present. It is changeable.
The squirrel is legion. American cities and their
squirrels are byproducts of industrialization—

The ability of wealthy colonists to realize their own
dreams for a closed system, divorced from existing
imperialisms. The production of goods (to sell, and
with which to fight) grew as humans moved beyond

Biological limits. Indigenous people, gray wolves, and
Lobsterbacks were marked for displacement
to eradicate the threats to a new empire—
an empire of American Squirrels. Change the city,

Change the squirrel. Commerce consolidated power.
Buildings scraped the sky. Agriculture went out.
Exit cattle. Exit sow.
Enter squirrel.

Sciurus Rex.

I.

Figure 2. Edwin Denby, Secretary of the Navy (1921–1924), feeds Pete the squirrel at the White House in October 1922. Original image caption: "When called to the White House to attend Cabinet meetings, officers of the Cabinet always remember Pete and bring him a few nuts." Library of Congress.

The Interrogation of Charlie Ferguson

Found poem

December 18, 1901

    Dear Sir— I respectfully
submit
    the following report of
        Charles Ferguson

—age 10   —white   —#302 C St. NW.

    At 1:30 this afternoon
    I caught the boy in the act

of <u>chasing squirrels</u>

in the N E part
    of the Capitol Grounds.

    He said he thought they were
                wild,
    and that he was
at liberty

    to catch or kill them if he could.
    I took him to the
Guard-Room

where he spent ¾ of an hour

    crying and promising
    "not to do it again"
    and to tell the other little boys

the squirrels were to be left alone.

    The parents gave the boy a severe chastising,

    which I think ought to keep him from troubling
the squirrels
    any more.

        Yours respectfully,
        A. F. Barrott

Squirrels of Washington I

Why do you dig so furtively? What are you looking for—
Something you hid before? Are you looking for
                              Your predator?

Do you ever find rest? Do you dream of treadmill forests—
Impenetrable burrows and nests?
                    Somewhere the sharp foxes

Can't get? Somewhere free?   Or, has your life in the city
Somehow become open to care ... the highest expression
      Of your deepest prayer?

Henrie Introduced

I met Henrie
in Kalorama in 2016,
black eyes watching my every move.
She said to me:

There hasn't been just one Henrie
but many. She cut her teeth
on Arbor Day, then
made a populist pivot
with William Jennings Bryan;
rode out Teapot Dome
in the judiciary; headed west
to spread the New Deal;
dined in Camelot
as humans launched to space;
hawked environmental
policy for Nixon; had a soft spot
in her heart for Geraldine Ferraro.

Kind squirrel, guiding
daemon, common soul
of Washington,
ambassador to the Capitol.
Tree specialist on behalf of
squirrel-kind serving
at the pleasure of
all creatures everywhere.

The Park for Little Wanderers

Henrie says "the park was made for me
    so that I won't have to go away."

A wall is growing in the park
    asking questions about the nature of things

    like *are you in*
        or *are you out?*

The Curators

undress in the shadows of
three-hundred years of American printmaking

letting down their tight scrim shrouds
pinned exquisitely against high white walls

of what they call the *most democratic medium*.
Cotton Mather looks down uncertainly

outing Audubon's bowing birds. Whistler's fog
hides a passionate lovers' embrace

of posthumous Pollock hacking from beyond
the grave a space for the inevitable Coca-Cola

model bottle nude bright shining skin exposed,
the pop-rubble shuttle of our ever-expanding universe.

Figure 3. "Orange-Bellied Squirrel," after John James Audubon (1780–1851); printed by John T. Bowen (1801–1856); hand-colored lithograph on wove paper; gift of Ella Solomon. Cooper Hewitt, Smithsonian Design Museum.

A Fashion of Birth

Washington, Washington, city of spring
generating new light

and out-of-state plates.
Henrie swears it is getting fuller every day

emphasizing the size of thighs.
She notices the domestic dangling

lanyards and key chains,
cameras strapped to tourists

clutching at scraps. Phone and charger
plying a set of restless fingers, slips

to the floor with a plastic chop, breaking
the spell; she locks eyes with the writer who

self-consciously knows he is now part of
the show. Henrie keenly feels

the capital curiosity she has become,
keeper of books, a park-sitter

stopper stuck somewhere
between Vermeer and van Gogh.

In the Public Garden

We have
left the heartland.
Today a thalia,
a muse, lays her head upon
a park bench and dreams.
Plastic bags a bounty
half-way down
the costal red-breast
robin
watching oblong
Monarchs
bump up
from the South
and away
creating
and joining
the migratory
stream.

Interregnum

Henrie—
the paper,
how it piles—
(grown wild)
    in this nook
deciphering the sky
speaking to the leaves
       through the wind.

Figure 4. front, Library of Congress reader card (2016)

Walking Home from the Library of Congress

Row on row. So many ways to say no. Don't
hurt the squirrels; Don't feed the squirrels;
And don't, whatever you do, don't let the squirrels
in to the Library of Congress. With books,
with a little knowledge, they would surely
be unstoppable.

> This card is not an official Government ID
>
> All readers wishing to use the Library's reading rooms or to request materials from the Library's collections must first register and obtain a Reader Identification Card. The Reader Identification Card is issued only to researchers who plan to use the Library's reading rooms and collections. Note: Additional entry criteria may be in force in various reading rooms.
>
> It is a violation of Federal Law and punishable by fine and/or imprisonment to steal or willfully damage or destroy Library books or other Library property.
>
> Telephone: 202-707-5000
> Telephone TTY: 202-707-6200
>
> **Library of Congress, Washington, D.C. 20540**

Figure 5. back, Library of Congress reader card (2016)

Recovery Day

Henrie watches the long day wane away
book pages fading into dusk like the shadow
line of the Mall reaching up to the Capitol.
A squirrel wrestles a pretzel from the can
unnoticed by a group of storky runners who
grab in tandem at their wrists to check
their stable mile-pace. Leisure, like running,
says Henrie (to no one in particular) isn't art
until you make it beautiful.

Henrie at Trashcan

Henrie detrained in Washington at two
purchasing with four dollar bills an ancient-grain baguette
and thereupon making like a happy Caesar from Union
up the Capitoline like a wolf to feast upon her kill.

And all that afternoon she paraded the parapets
of Smithson's kingdom observing military exercises,
tearing off fleshy chunks of bread like angel cake
before duly sacrificing the final stump to the squirrels.

Vertiginous

Henrie says
humans have words
squirrels don't have
because the words
describe feelings
squirrels can
never
know.

II.

Figure 6. Caspar Wolf, "Architectural Fantasy of Antique Ruins with a Watermill, 1760s." Gouache on laid paper. National Gallery of Art.

Watermill

The rivers thawed in March that year,
seasons churning round around
like cumbersome wooden spokes.

We hid in one of the sheltered corners
on the low floor of Peirce's grist mill,
listening to the water rushing
chutting through the watermill.

Steady rain had fallen for weeks,
peltering the hard earth before gathering
and rolling down to join the flow.

The wheel turned faster
as water moved more urgently every day,
descending from the tearing hillsides
of dark vales and hidden gorges.

We were alive with a pressure that swelled
and ran wild through the northern woods
surging and spreading in search of open spaces.

It beat and crashed like a roaring anger
among the rocks, a nervous tic, a shiver
in your knees, that fluttered in the dark

and fell like your fingers, in my back.
The searing tip of your nose
powering my cheek
like water so hot it feels cold.

I Worked at Lady's on Wednesday

I worked at Lady's on Wednesday laying out and scheduling the upcoming month and texted some people to make dinner plans—chatted with a friend about law school for a half hour then went out at 8:30 for a night run—glorious run—it was cool and cloudy, the type of suspended cloud that lights up with ambient offshoots and doesn't fog or prohibit vision but just illuminates.

I ran down Vermont to Lafayette Park and passed down the west side of the White House continuing on to the Washington Monument, then cut back toward Lincoln. I passed the WWII Memorial and the evening tourists wearing green and red glow sticks, flashing the stone walls with iPhone flashing—the path along the reflecting pool is military-precision straight.

I went up the steps to Abe's house, Rocky style, topping the steps beside outposts of young couples looking back east, eyes alight—I thought of the Dream ("tell them about the dream, Martin...") as I departed the steps—I ran with a red flashing bike light in my left hand and still I snuck up on people unintentionally and made them jump—I took that as a compliment to the low impact of my running stride—then back to the base of Washington's monument and on to the Smithsonian Castle, beside the late-night dog jogger who bounded down the path like a sleigh captain, keeping time with his two white labs.

I darted unsmartly in front of two cars while crossing Fifth—they hit their brakes and honked, a bit dramatically—I raised my hand to them to say sorry, but continued riding on the high of my run flow—one loop of the fox den on Capitol Hill and back down to the less-impressive wading pool where Ulysses S. Grant hangs out—silent ducks lay tucked into the recessed marble molding of the basin one snapping its head around to check me out while the others slept on.

Two cab drivers chatted standing between their two parked cars, taking in the night waiting for a call or perhaps not caring for work after a long day or before a generous night—back past the Gallery where I had toured earlier in the day—the still sculptures in the garden like a memory of dinosaurs waiting to be discovered—another runner, a couple strolling back to their car, mud puddles in the low divots of the dirt.

Traffic blocked my path back to the Washington Monument and, rather than break my stride, I cut north toward Constitution and the building where the Constitution lives, three-hundred-and-twenty-something breezy years of parchment and ink—I cut west again, to the Ellipse, up to the Corcoran and Executive Building, Farragut Square, flying up Connecticut now, drops of rain alighting gently on my temples.

I'm meeting Lady at 9:50 and I'm timing it just right—fly past stores, fly past bars, fly past empty offices being turned over one room at a time—my phone tells me I'm approaching ten miles. Lady calls and asks where I am. I start calling out the numbers of the houses I pass each one getting closer until I can see Lady standing there on the sidewalk. Kiss. Pant. Stop.

House Money

> "No sufficient governmental interest justifies limits on the
> political speech of nonprofit or for-profit corporations."
> —"Citizens United" (2010)

Little things are the war,
not merely a matter of bullion

to sustain a moving army:
the imperial nature

of our very own ideas
how sure we are

of our own world;
I am uncomfortable in the world

as you know it is—
I don't always like the patterns

infused with your personality
which I reject reflexively

as it challenges my understanding
of what is possible

not everything but rather
tightening circles of precision

ending up together we
are dealers, common schemers.

Untitled

> *And yet there's One whose gently holding hands*
> *let this falling fall and never land.*
> —Rilke

Through the city one journal entry
one blue word at a time,
multigrain bread and a Bosc pear.
Thank you, self-check-out machine.
I walked down Ninth as the clouds turned to mist
and then discernable drops.
I stopped at the atrium to wash and eat my fruit,
having eaten half of the bread on the way.
Umbrellas went from dangling to tonight and aloft.

The scrim leaves of the arbor canopy
define domestic energy
for eight weeks before the squirrels
are turned
out of the nests. Leaves
come down anyway.

The Loop

Land of superhighways
over-laned like razor blades
cutting down five times
one wide red line of un-
coincidental growth

traveling along the
superhighway in the sky,
bounding perch to perch
with unknown nonchalance.
Henrie could not have known
how amazing she was,
how unnecessary the leap,
the ten-foot drop, the dramatic flop,
the branch she brought to its taught point
dragged brazenly down to the next exit.

Figure 7. "Squirrel Cage," c. 1875. Original caption from the Luce Center: "A squirrel cage is any cage with a cylindrical framework that allows small animals to run inside it. This piece, with its elaborate turret, flag, and windows, was likely used for entertainment. The owner probably trained small animals to perform tricks, then charged people a small fee to watch the show." Smithsonian American Art Museum.

H Street

On this morning early in spring
you and I walk the dogs down rows of brick
and brownstones, pausing in the shade
of first magnolias and first church.
The curious ones scrounge around
the dependable hydrant with preternatural
snouts, alert to every windblown thing
reading mail in subtle delight. Intently
you scan the sidewalk for the debris
of occupied four-legged lives. As you stoop
to collect, your body becomes to me
the geography of care. I wonder
at its depth, where you're going, the spot
where we might sit and watch the stars
carve gracefully across the universe.
You call out my name, calling me back
to the dogs' full rasping, their exuberance,
your contrapposto. You drum your finger
and the restless pair falls silent for a moment,
agape. Then you dash off and they lunge behind
bounding after you in the brisk air
heavy with irrepressible budding. And
there I go after you—my love on a leash, loosened,
tracking the place where our hope and heart
meet, borne aloft and breathless, bearing
the beautiful weight of our world.

Squirrels of Washington II

> *The Eastern gray squirrel, a shakedown artist*
> *as aggressive as any three-card monte hustler.*
> —John Kelly

Rodents: evolutionary success with chiseling teeth
and high reproducible rates. More than 2,000 species,
they are by far the largest group of living mammals.
65 million years ago a meteor hit the Earth—70%
of the Earth's animals died. Some mammals survived
and adapted to a changing Earth.

Mammals: — hair

      — ear bone for special hearing

      — milk producing

I moved through the usual green spaces, but there
is a void of activity. The rain? The rodents have resigned
their field to the bounty of the birds feasting on the ignorance
of the worms. I retreat from the weather into the gallery
again for lack of fresh territory. I look for squirrels in the paintings
and prints. Ducks and other winged creatures abound. Not
a squirrel to be found. Foxes, turtles, bears, and doves.
Why not bring the scurrying survivor to the foreground?

Seeing the same prints a second day in a row
they have been transformed overnight into artifacts.

Arc Welders at Night

after Martin Lewis

Two masked workmen
with backs to the vantage
look down upon the fiery track
of trolley illuminated
by blinding torches
shielded by a cardboard stand.
The escaping light from two points
create a Cartesian
crown of thorns, the road
made new in time for morning.
Women walk across the way, toeing
the electric cables
running to a hidden source:
drypoint and sandground.
Manhole covers and iron cranes,
windows set to *lookout*
on the working world,
said the women
turning toe to the beggar
we cannot fully see:
the last shadow left
as all the blinds go down.

Figure 8. Thumbnail from "Arc Welders at Night," 1937 by Martin Lewis (1881–1962). National Gallery of Art.

Lafayette Park

> *The density of squirrels in that park
> is the highest ever recorded in the scientific literature.*
> —David Manski

Influence is a matter of altitude
black eyes survey the amplitude
of activity in the Great Gray Capitol
on H Street. There must be one-hundred
squirrels in that small square now—
they're just shredding the trees.

Space High

There are places without walls
you don't have to tell me
or keep the secret of space
where one can go for days—
space is measured in all directions
and I move on slopes.

The high of leaping loosed
arches and tangled curves of air.

I regroup to high spaces to make up
for the latitude of horses and
automobile and

I will make my way
out to the greatness beyond.

Aerial Artist

Henrie says rooftops &
cupolas come with it,
and scaffolding the same.
Parapets build up to it—
pigeons slightly perched
can take the tingles.
Crowded moldings,
cornice caps and shingles
project themselves into the air . . .
and disappear.

Henrie's Favorite

My favorite one
    reads newspapers in the park
and tucks the folded pages under his arm
with finality. I love the resolute breath,
the downward glance that lingers, his mind
moving at a respectable speed as it synchronizes.

I   study the cantilevered cranes
shouldering up buildings like an overseer.

Down here in the park,
hovering above
I know that my favorite
    loves me back.

Sometimes I Make Lists Because I Don't Want to Forget Anything

> *A single squirrel can bury up to three-thousand nuts in a season in a process known as caching. It can store nuts across dozens of locations and even spatially organize them by type. They bury food in winter caches using a method called scatter hoarding and locate these caches using memory and smell.*
> —Emma Bryce

  Arbor nuts, flowers breaking buds.
Oaks! Hickory, pecan, walnut,
and beech. Oh, elm, maple, mulberry.
  Hackberry and horse chestnuts
the falling cartography of survival.

Figure 9. World War I, War Bonds Poster, 1917. Original posters were accompanied by a small sheet printed with a children's story, "The Squirrel," advising children to buy thrift stamps, and instructing the teacher to post the story near the poster. Library of Congress.

Emelia

In a loose blue shirt, she feeds eight pigeons
and five smaller birds from a plastic bag she keeps tucked
under her arm.

The birds strut in slow circles pecking at macadam
peeling off from the spot one by one, whispering
solemnly *nothing to see here. nothing to see here.* The smaller
more-agile birds grab the biggest chunks and decamp smartly
 to an out-of-sight cache.

It's time to go.
The trees are full and dropping helicopters.

Hymns For Rachel

after Genesis 29

Verse I.
Everything begins
in the mountains,
core peaks
harbor the truths
we seek
forever unfurling
eternal tapestries
from the skies,
colors and signs,
fall to the ocean.
Even the promise
of love must move
ever farther
from its source.

Verse II.
Hidden on the far
shore, shuttling,
scorching, is the future
wreathed in
botanical sunshine.
It promises to keep
nothing but brevity,
a journey of one-
million rain clouds
could not subdue the
 river. Krishna seeking
radha seeking krishna
brings the shores
closer together.

Verse III.
Visions of you
in city under
snow on snow,
the wiling river
runs wild below
the icy sheath
I go to the sea
to the sea I go
unsleeping, never
slowing, on and on
for a chance of you
I'll bed my head
on a rock for years
for years of you.

Verse IV.
I concede to stop
when this is over,
I agree to sleep
for seven years,
a relative rock pusher
can't explain the reason,
doesn't mean
he won't try. I
didn't come to
wrestle god,
or become both
the dreamer and the dream,
but life is a river and
we end where we begin.

III.

Figure 10. Plumbago sp., National Museum of Natural History, plant image collection.

Plumbago

A Puritan incursion, a bluish-gray
aberration, fainter than clair de lune,
paler and greener than the dusk
obstructing the progress of the night
makes landfall—
clair de lune, light of the moon,
carbon, castor, French, gull,

hathi, iron, plumbeous, plumbago,
charcoal, argent, arsenic, cadet,
battleship, cinerous, auro, ash,
stormcloud, trolley, taupe, timberwolf,
stone, slate, silver sand, silver, Roman
silver, platinum, pewter, Payne's gray,
manatee, hoar, gainsboro, feldgrau, dim,
granite rain,

Seafarers now slipping into focus
on the shore,
a chiaroscuro

of arms and feet unfurling

after months of nothing
but a bit of wavecrest, albatross, and dried salt,

stretching out fingertips

of smoke
to draw firm plans

in the sand.

The Squirrel is Legion

The story of squirrels
is one of conqueror

before Alexander (that upright commander)
was even a dander

in the first Neanderthal eye
with the same stay and banter,

hole punchers and sky swillers reigned,
chipper skillers—limited

marching-parts, but
infinitely agile.

Animal Desire

An atlas of an animal's desire
goes through its dram,
nest or tree, nook
or underground lair
and circles out from there
on ships
ferreted under auspice of discretion
into bourbon cask chambers.
The warm buzz
of a suggestive glance,
something behind wild eyes,
a flexibility of the heart
declined in *prima sutra*
good for jumping
vulnerable to words
and the word that shapes
to second position from the extreme
of a wheel,
a posessive declension.

My First Summer in the Silicon

for John Muir

The startup is in haste to get rich,
        and often does, now that keeping contractors

costs nothing. No housing, HR, or office space.
        These big sheep-owners keep

their global flock at slight expense. Large profits are
        realized, the money invested is eternally returned.

But satisfaction is the rarest formation. Anything thus
        quickly acquired, usually creates a desire for more.

Cubs Win World Series, Four Games to Three

Henrie went for
        a walk down to

        the Navy Yard, a misnomer,
while she walked

it was probable
        that the passage of time

        continued in all areas
even outside her observation. Just like

the president
        is usually in DC but with periodic

        departures for security purposes.
She walked and accepted this

even while tempted
        to believe otherwise, to believe that only her

        reality was real, a supremely creative
creator composing news stories

about possible events
        happening out of her time.

        Finding ways to pull
a coherent narrative together.

Coffee

> *I have measured out my life with coffee spoons.*
> —J. Alfred Prufrock

I would give my last dollar every time
(count to ten) just to look at my face
(reflecting the oil-spill swirls and swamp steam)
in my black cup (and guzzle to the dregs
my graven image). The laws of science apply
the illuminated feeling of my mind (but lightly).
This benevolent oil spill hugs my throat. I once saw a man
suspend a cup—give a buck—to the rough life
in the bean shop. I did the first few times
too many ideas at once. Decide later if they are any good.
Turn the spoon—I measure
the quality of what I find in the clock-wise slipstream.

Christopher Wren Dances in Anacostia

one, two,
red lines, foot falls
running interference.

three, four,
defunct housing fund
for the birds
of SE Washington.

Metrophysics

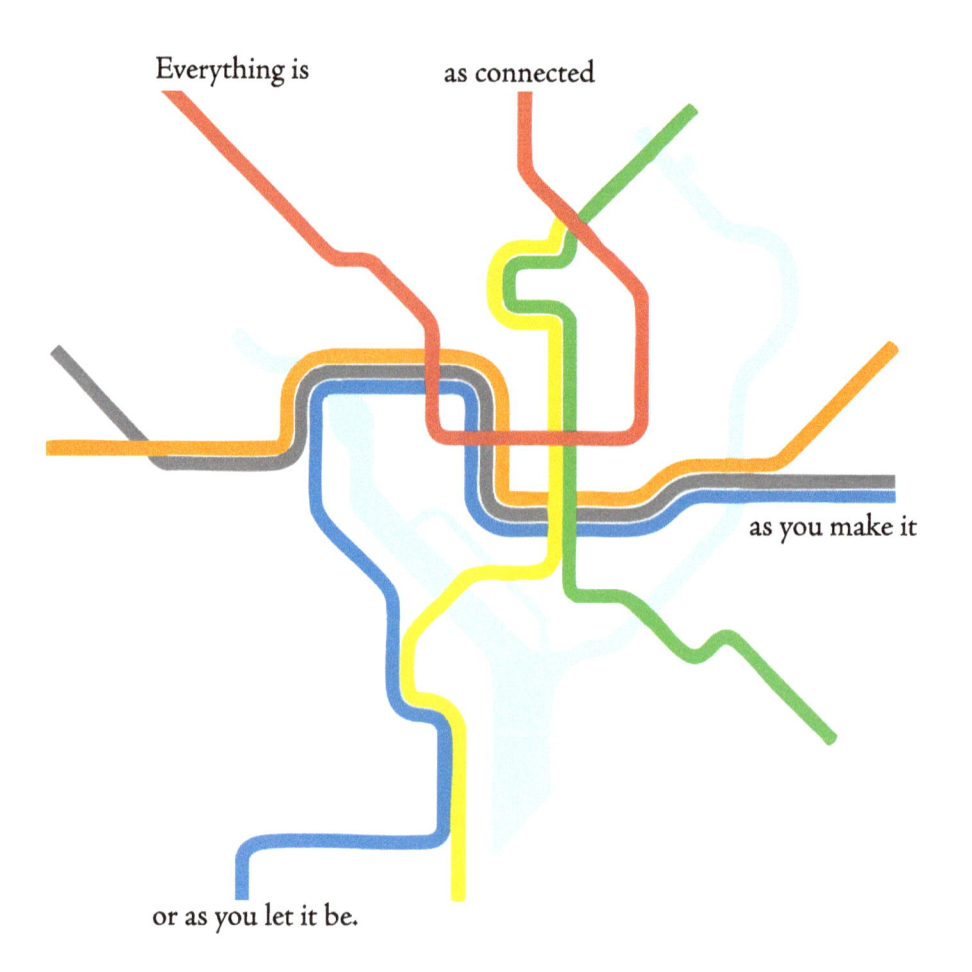

Everything is as connected

as you make it

or as you let it be.

Squirrels of Washington III

Unnamed park
in the crux of a turn on

New Jersey, NW.
The territory of silver-tailed squirrels:

    splotchy, like the creator flicked acid.

Greater Than Me

Intuition understands the tree
bark succumbing to the claw
and a canopy thicker than the rain.

But faculties of observation fail
and miss the fact of a real tree
whose many parts are greater than me.

Capitol Hill Classic

The high branch (sycamore?) from which to watch
west, or peek northeast around the window frame, and observe
the exchanges that kill and botch across the country—
kill, as in "you're killing this"—*you are absolutely
killing this*—botch, as in bungle, as in without care—
you absolutely botched this and the country is headed south—
people in this country get what they deserve. Henrie talked
with Elizabeth and Jocelyn when they got back from the gym,
ran to the Navy Yard (3.5 miles) to pick up a race number
(1928). Bought two bananas, two pints of blueberries (buy one,
get one), and twenty-four ounces of yellow Powerade.
Just another Friday (the thirteenth) in the high perch.

Offshoots

H— hid in the willow stalks of the unnamed park
on New Jersey to feel the stalks brush against her face
and move between this world and the next—drawing
the attention of the spikier squirrels vibrating frenetically
on sugar dropped by the blue-shirted Russian grandmother
brewing morning tea for three, the Virgin Mother and me.

Radio Waves

Henrie sits on her preferred perch, the top floor
of the Dunbar Theater, flipped to play the apartment—
watching outer buildings stretch into the red light
(copper tops alight with a soft clocktower glow)
she can hear the amplified whisper of two brothers
cackling, husky murmurators about carburetors
and the hilarity of our general disrepair.

Hypotheosis

strobes on
descending blue
broken time
great smoke ascension
blinding seekers—
the truth
would die for truth
would die way out there
so saxophone drone
so day-time nightclub
divine elide
right to rhythm
everything seems to rhyme
everything seems to rhyme.

Proof of the poet
is not proof of the poetry
water wine
left behind
roll stone
the gardener knows
sound vines
snaking purple
snaking purple sound vines
into endless heaven.

(Jo-Lonn) Dunbar Theater

> *While the squirrel in his gambols*
> *Fearless round about me ambles,*
> *As if he were bent on showing*
> *In my kingdom he'd a share;*
> —Paul Dunbar, "Nutting Song"

The world is your theater.

Act 1:
running
never dogged it
didn't bag the last 10 yards.

Act 2:
visceral balance
and reflexive kindness,
a class act
every season.

Act 3:
dreaming
of an impish dance
till the very break of dawn.

I'll Be Seeing You (Henrie's Song)

November cold the first sip of morning water
from the pipes that run beneath the streets.
I stand at the window to see the light
running away though the unkept branches.
I cherish the branches I have known.
This day is an unexpected beginning.

Election

after Luke 22

The people in town walk to the polls
north and south side between them a line
dividing those who have visions
and those who see the world for what it is.
I once saw a woman standing at the end of my bed
she said get up and get in your car
and drive until you get to Utica.
Give all your cash to the first child you see
on Memorial Parkway and then go
to a coffee shop and explain how you have no money
but that you would like a coffee if they have
some to spare. If they give you a coffee,
tell them the story of the woman at your bed. If they don't
give you a coffee yell the first thing that comes into your mind
and run out the door into Utica
to start your new life there.

Compilation

Bike ride winter
I have one vague collapsing sense
of a scrapbook flipping ride through dreams
last night I dreamt of differentiation. The lack of me causes
wonder, pause. Again, riding Uber Pool shotgun
home on election night. The archetypal destination
Plato's cave-in on Chestnut Hill Parkway,
the bench where I left a gram of passion
still running for my life. One winter bike
on election night
to bring selves together.

Mrs. Frisby and the Rats

It's mostly dark. Foreboding
(rodents in media get a bad rap)
shots of rain and magic spitzle. The mouse,
we see, is on a mission to save her child.

Traceur[1]

I remember the   bright Frenchman
a neon tracjack   zipping down the
city stucco
                        walls, an excitable
crunching footstep   shuttlecocking rooftops
like an old-school   slalom
champ veering   blindly through the
city without skis.   Tickling trashcans
unaware. The   swatting hipster pilgrim
had only just   arrived this morning
on iron   horseback.

He's in the   kitchen now
proselytizing on   behalf of the unseen stars.
I catch a hard   quotient of his religion
so we go together
into a reality of   white-night house music
all night high   on matcha and desire
                        for the human skin
touching down   on my skin. The rattling ripple
of the river bass   shaking bones. I'm at home
snaking through
the sleepless   cathedral night
victory bounding
                        the vertical jungle
dubbing   piddler prophets
of the urban   you and me.

---

1   one who participates in parkour; a free runner.

The Machine

says *I hear that you are hurting*
and I hear and understand that you are worried
about the future for your family
and I can do something about it
and the machine drones on, automaton
then it killed the soldier at the gate
they say *it's hiding out among the trees*
and we have to find it has to be stopped
oh, wow, they've got the machine
and are dragging the machine through the streets
and now the machine is trying to say something
and the people are giving it space to speak, listen now
it says *I hear that you are hurting*
and I hear and understand that you are worried
about the future for your family
and I can do something about it
and the machine drones on, automaton
pay attention to see what it does now
the question that will be discovered
is whether the machine is hypocritical
oh, wow, it didn't take long for the machine
to convince the people who are not of one mind
to listen to what the machine has to say.

Imperfect Mirror

Standing at the   high peak of the bridge
You lean to see   the sailboat cross below,
Below yet another   bridge below for trains.
They disappear   forever into the underpass
They disappear   forever into the undertow
Leaving empty   echoes from the other side
The other side of   the bridge remains out of sight
of the other side   of the bridge
Where the tacking   could have resumed.
Where the tracking   could have resumed.
I would have left   you there
Had it not been   for the fire in your hair
I would have left   you there
Had it not been   for the deferral
The cobalt city   turning to fire
In a moment   taken by the night
But for now   I can see nothing
Except the sunlight   in your hair.

In A Different Key, Gatsby

We have come to accept that some things
must happen in their own way.
Myrtal was a love I loved to hate,
now in pieces, feeling spurned
on the Long I interstate. Her husband,
my friend Wilson, he's dead too—
badly played like dirty piano keys.
The remaining few, we live around here.
On the outskirts of real striving for unattainable. Lights
in the distance are sometimes enough to keep us.
In flats so drab they reject our very being. We don't
spend our time. Wisely we dream big, we tip the kid,
we take long drives to the city and turn around again.
We stumble out into the night, grabbing at air
and water, to pull our friend from the cool waters of the pool
where he is down circling round
the soft currents we wish he would survive
every time, it ends like this.

My Dear Sir

Found poem

I assume you are not aware of the fact,
(but it is a fact)
that the squirrels in the Capitol grounds
(while somewhat amusing)
are nevertheless a nuisance in several respects.

In the first place, they drive away the birds
(by robbing their nests)
and the birds are far more useful
in destroying the insects that infest the trees.

In the second place, they are a nuisance
(to the residents in the vicinity).
A few years ago I planted a tree
(an English walnut) in my backyard
which has been bearing three or four years.

Since the squirrels have been there,
(the squirrels take the nuts)
I have not been able to save any of the nuts
(before they are fairly ripe).

The squirrels are about the place nearly every day
(and on Thanksgiving day one of them
sat on my porch railing and looked at me
as I sat at my desk, as imprudent
as anything could be, as much as to say,
how can you help yourself!).

I don't want to kill or injure them,
(but I must protect myself in some way).
I beg to suggest that you send them to the
Old Soldiers' Home, where they will be
equally amusing, have more trees,
and harm no one. Respectfully yours.
                    W. I. Dodge

December 4, 1905

America's Front Yard: An Echo

                        Henrie looked up at me, tilted her head a degree
          and asked, pointedly after a pause, "What is this?
What have we been doing here?"

     "Why all this running around?"

"Why poetry? Why books?"
                                   "I am just a squirrel."

   "I roam, I soar, I thrive, I survive."

"You're not going to fix anything . . ." she said,

       " . . . spending time with me."
                    I said, "There is a wall growing in the park"

"Asking questions about the nature of things,"

    "*In or out?*   I will answer: 'a tree.'"

"I want to be free, running up with you above the wall
                       shuttling through the canopy . . ."

"back and forth, back and forth . . . where I want to be."

        "The park was made for us"
     "so that we can be"
                      "American squirrels."

Figure 13. H. Lyman Saÿen, "Trees," c. 1912–1914, oil on canvas. Smithsonian American Art Museum. This artwork is a gift of H. Lyman Saÿen to his nation.

Notes

The book's epigraph comes from a 1903 letter sent by George A. Gustin to the superintendent of US Capitol grounds, Elliott Woods, asking assistance for the squirrels with winter approaching. In the early US there were only three departments—State, Treasury, and War—to carry out all federal programs. George Gustin of Treasury worked in public health and marine hospital fields. This letter has been archived by the Architect of the Capitol, https://www.aoc.gov/sites/default/files/squirrels_gustin_19031107.pdf

"American Squirrel" includes an epigraph from Etienne Benson, "The Urbanization of the Eastern Gray Squirrel in the United States," *Journal of American History* 100, no. 3 (2013): 692, http://www.jstor.org/stable/44308759.

"The Interrogation of Charlie Ferguson" is a found poem drawing on a letter sent by US Capitol policeman A. F. Barrott to his captain, J. P. Megrew, on December 19, 1901. This letter has been archived by the Architect of the Capitol, https://www.aoc.gov/sites/default/files/squirrels_barrott_19011218.pdf.

"Henry Introduced" references the creation of Arbor Day. For a summary of Arbor Day's founding in the context of American environmentalism, read Jill Lepore, "Root and Branch," *New Yorker*, May 29, 2023. (The online title is "What We Owe Our Trees.")

"The Curators" and **"Arc Welders at Night"** were written at the National Gallery of Art during the exhibit "Three Centuries of American Prints" which ran from April 3 to June 24, 2016. "Arc Welders at Night" is a print by Martin Lewis. See Judith Brodie et al., *Three Centuries of American Prints: From the National Gallery of Art* (Thames & Hudson, 2016).

"Watermill" was first published in *Clarion*, Spring 2010.

"House Money" includes an epigraph from the majority opinion of the Supreme Court case "Citizens United v. Federal Elections Commission" (2010), written by Justice Anthony Kennedy.

"Untitled" includes an epigraph from the poem "Herbst" by Rainer Maria Rilke in which "Und doch ist Einer, welcher dieses Fallen / unendlich sanft in seinen Händen hält" is translated as "And yet there's One whose gently holding hands / let this falling fall and never land" by William H. Gass, *Reading Rilke: Reflections on the Problems of Translation* (Knopf, 1999), 35. There are many English translations of this Rilke poem. This one is my very favorite.

"Squirrels of Washington II" includes an epigraph from *Washington Post* journalist John Kelly. Kelly reports that Lafayette Square, just north of the White House, is the site researchers believe to have been "the highest density of squirrels ever recorded in scientific literature: roughly 20 squirrels per acre." The last lines of my poem borrow from a statement in the article from National Park Service ranger Bill Ruback made to *the Post* in 1977: "There must be 100 squirrels in that small square now, and they're just shredding the trees." I like the visceral scene and soundscape the word shredding evokes. Kelly is the creator and purveyor of "Squirrel Week," an annual April celebration of squirrel life in Washington, DC. John Kelly, "Remembering the Great Squirrel Purge of Lafayette Square," *Washington Post*, April 10, 2016.

"Lafayette Park" includes an epigraph by David Manski, an urban wildlife biologist for the National Park Service who closely watched the lives of squirrels in Washington's Lafayette Park in the early 1980s. Manski estimated there were about 125 squirrels in the park during the period of his study. Manski qtd. in George Clifford, "Squirrels, Friends Go Nuts in Their 'Digs' at Lafayette Square," *Washington Post*, June 20, 1984.

"Sometimes I Make Lists Because I Don't Want to Forget Anything" includes an epigraph by environmental journalist Emma Bryce. It describes the squirrel's practice of caching food in order to survive the winter. Emma Bryce, "Do Squirrels Remember Where They Buried Their Nuts?," *Scientific American*, November 20, 2023.

"My First Summer in the Silicon" is a twenty-first century reimagining of a line from John Muir's "My First Summer in the Sierra" (1911) in which Muir writes of his 1869 travels: "The California sheepowner is in haste to get rich, and often does, now that pasturage costs nothing, while the climate is so favorable that no winter food supply, shelter-pens, or barns are required. Therefore large flocks may be kept at slight expense, and large profits realized, the money invested doubling, it is claimed, every other year. This quickly acquired wealth usually creates desire for more." John Muir, My First Summer in the Sierra, (Houghton Mifflin, 1911), 30.

"Coffee" includes an epigraph from T. S. Eliot, *Prufrock and Other Observations* (The Egoist Ltd., 1917), 12.

"Christopher Wren Dances in Anacostia" imagines a modern-day Christopher Wren (1632–1723)—an influential architect who favored long boulevards and circles with streets coming off like spokes—flitting unthinkingly through the modern-day south-east part of the capital city. Wren caused Pierre L'Enfant and other designers of Washington, DC, to emulate the aesthetics of London and other European cities in their planning. Pamela Scott, "Designing the Nation's Capital,"

National Park Service, March 9, 2002. www.nps.gov/
parkhistory/online_books/ncr/designing-capital/sec3.htm.
The wren illustration is by the author.

"Metrophysics" is a word sculpture incorporating a
vector image of the Washington Metro system designed
by digitally tracing a public domain map of the public
transportation system.

"Hypotheosis" is a portmanteau of the words hypothesis
and apotheosis; a best guess about something ordinary
becoming divine.

"(Jo-Lonn) Dunbar Theater" includes an epigraph from
the poem "Nutting Song" by Paul Dunbar, *The Complete
Poems of Paul Laurence Dunbar* (Dodd, Mead, and Company, 1913), 282. The last lines of the poem also reference
Dunbar's poem "The Corn-Stalk Fiddle": "So the night goes
on and the dance is o'er, / And the merry girls are homeward gone, / But I see it all in my sleep once more, / And I
dream till the very break of dawn / Of an impish dance on
a red-hot griddle / To the screech and scrape of a corn-stalk
fiddle." Dunbar, *Complete Poems*, 16–17.

"Election" emulates the language of Jesus' cryptic
instructions to his disciples in Chapter 22 of Luke's gospel.
The title "Election" refers both to election day (November
8, 2016) and the nuanced and complex Calvinist belief
that certain individuals ("the elect") are predestined for
salvation.

"Mrs. Frisby and the Rats" is an allusion to Robert C.
O'Brien's book *Mrs. Frisby and the Rats of NIMH* (1971)
which was made into a movie of the same name (1982).
The book raises questions about where and what places

creatures call home, as the titular mouse, Mrs. Frisby, makes hard decisions about how to save her son Timothy.

"In a Different Key, Gatsby" invokes the plot of F. Scott Fitzgerald, *The Great Gatsby* (Charles Scribner's Sons, 1925).

"My Dear Sir" is a found poem drawing on another letter to the superintendent of the US Capitol grounds, Elliott Woods, who seems to have spent much of his career engaged in squirrel-related business. Nimbyist W. I. Dodge, "attorney and solicitor of patents," writes to Woods asking to have the squirrels around the Capitol removed to the Soldiers Home, north of the Capitol (today a national monument also home to President Lincoln's Cottage). This letter has been archived by the Architect of the Capitol, https://www.aoc.gov/sites/default/files/dodge.pdf.

"America's Front Yard: An Echo" attempts to close this collection of poetry with several callbacks to previous poems. The artwork on the facing page is pre-war painting by the Philadelphian H. Lyman Saÿen who worked as an artists and scientist throughout his career; among Saÿen's inventions were a new type of X-ray tube, and a steel billiard ball. Much of his artwork is in the public domain.

Index

A

Alexander III (King of Macedonia) 48
Anacostia 53
Arbor Day 8
Audubon, John James 10

B

bananas 57
bears 31
Benson, Etienne (historian) 1
bicycles 24, 64
birds 10, 31, 40, 70
   albatross 47
   bald eagle 1
   doves 31
   duck 31
   pigeon 36, 40
   robin 13
   wren 53
blueberries 57
books 12
Bryan, William Jennings 8
Bryce, Emma (journalist) 38

C

caching 38, 40
Caesar 17
Camelot 8
canopy 27, 72
Capitol, The 5, 8, 16, 24, 34, 70
Chicago Cubs 51
Citizens United (court case) 26
coffee 52, 63
Constitution, The 25

D

dancing 61
Descartes, René 32
dinosaurs 25
dogs 24, 30
Dunbar, Paul Laurence 61
Dunbar Theater 59

E

echoes 72

F

Farragut Square 25
Ferraro, Geraldine 8
Fitzgerald, F. Scott 69
flowers 46
foxes 7, 31
Frisby (literary mouse) 65
fruit 27

G

Gatsby, Jay (literary character) 69
Grant, Ulysses S. 24

H

heaven 60
helicopters 40
Henrie 8, 9, 12, 14, 16, 17, 18, 28, 36, 37, 51, 57, 59, 62, 72
highways 28
horse chestnuts 38
horses 35, 66
H Street 30, 34

I

insects
   Monarch butterfly 13

J

Jackson, Mahalia 24

K

Kalorama (neighborhood) 8
Kelly, John (journalist) 31
King, Martin Luther, Jr. 24

L

Lafayette Park 24, 34
leaves 14, 27
Lewis, Martin (printmaker) 32
Library of Congress 4, 14, 15
Lincoln, Abraham 24
Long Island, NY 69

M

mammals 1, 31
Manski, David (wildlife biologist) 34
Mather, Cotton 10
Metro, The 54
migration 13
Muir, John 50
Muses 13
music 66

N

National Gallery of Art xii, 22, 33
National Portrait Gallery 31
Navy Yard 51, 57
neanderthals 48
nests 7
newspapers 37
Nixon 8
nuts 4, 38, 61, 70

P

parkour 66
parks 9, 13, 34, 37, 58, 72
Peirce's Mill (Rock Creek) 23
piano 69
Plato 64
poetry 60, 72
Pollock, Jackson 10
prayer 7
Prufrock, J. Alfred 52
Puritans 47

R

radio 59
rain 23, 25, 27
religion 66
Rilke, Rainer Maria 27
Rocky (Balboa) 24
rodents 31
running 16, 24, 72

S

saxophone 60
scatter hoarding 38
ships 47, 49
  sailboat 68
Silicon Valley 50
Smithsonian 11, 17, 24, 29, 73
squirrels 1, 5, 6, 8, 11, 16, 17, 18, 27, 31, 34, 48, 55, 58, 61, 70, 72

T

tea 58
Teapot Dome 8
Thalia 13
theater 61
trees 49, 62, 71, 72, 73
  beech 38

elm 38
English walnut 70
hackberry 38
hickory 38
magnolia 30
maple 38
mulberry 38
oaks 38
pecan 38
sycamore 57
walnut 38
turtles 31

U

Utica, NY 63

V

van Gogh, Vincent 12
Vermeer, Johannes 12
Virgin Mary 58

W

walls 9, 10, 24, 35, 66, 72
Washington, DC 7, 8, 12, 17, 24, 25, 31, 51, 53
Washington Monument 24, 25
watermill 23
Whistler, James 10
White House 24
wolves 17
World Series 51
Wren, Christopher 53

Index of First Lines

A Puritan incursion, a bluish-gray, 47
An atlas of an animal's desire, 49
Arbor nuts, flowers breaking buds, 38

Bike ride winter, 64

December 18, 1901, 5

Everything begins, 41
Everything is as connected, 54

H— hid in the willow stalks of the unnamed park, 58
Henrie—, 14
Henrie detrained in Washington at two, 17
Henrie looked up at me, tilted her head a degree, 72
Henrie says, 18
Henrie says rooftops &, 36
Henrie says "the park was made for me, 9
Henrie sits on her preferred perch, the top floor, 59
Henrie watches the long day wane away, 16
Henrie went for, 51

I assume you are not aware of the fact, 70
I met Henrie, 8
I remember the bright Frenchman, 66
I worked at Lady's on Wednesday laying out and scheduling the, 24
I would give my last dollar every time, 51
In a loose blue shirt, she feeds eight pigeons, 40
Influence is a matter of altitude, 32
Intuition understands the tree, 56
It's mostly dark. Foreboding, 65

Land of superhighways, 28
Little things are the war, 26

My favorite one, 37

November cold the first sip of morning water, 62

On this morning early in spring, 30
one, two, 52

Rodents: evolutionary success with chiseling teeth, 31
Row on row. So many ways to say no. Don't, 15

says I hear that you are hurting, 67
Standing at the high peak of the bridge, 68
strobes on, 60

The bald eagle is an imperfect American, 1
The high branch (sycamore?) from which to watch, 56
The people in town walk to the polls, 63
The rivers thawed in March that year, 23
The startup is in haste to get rich, 50
The story of squirrels, 48
The world is your theater, 57
There are places without walls, 35
Through the city one journal entry, 27
Two masked workmen, 32

Undress in the shadows of, 10
Unnamed park, 55

Washington, Washington, city of spring, 12
We have, 13
We have come to accept that some things, 69
Why do you dig so furtively? What are you looking for, 7